CAMBRIDGE PRIMARY
Mathematics

Skills Builder

Name: _____

Contents

Cherri Moseley and Janet Rees

CAMBRIDGE
UNIVERSITY PRESS

CAMBRIDGE
UNIVERSITY PRESS

University Printing House, Cambridge CB2 8BS, United Kingdom

One Liberty Plaza, 20th Floor, New York, NY 10006, USA

477 Williamstown Road, Port Melbourne, VIC 3207, Australia

4843/24, 2nd Floor, Ansari Road, Daryaganj, Delhi – 110002, India

79 Anson Road, #06–04/06, Singapore 079906

Cambridge University Press is part of the University of Cambridge.

It furthers the University's mission by disseminating knowledge in the pursuit of education, learning and research at the highest international levels of excellence.

www.cambridge.org
Information on this title: education.cambridge.org/9781316509142

© Cambridge University Press 2016

First published 2016
20 19 18 17 16 15 14 13

Printed in Italy by Rotolito S.p.A.

A catalogue record for this publication is available from the British Library

ISBN 978-1-316-50914-2 Paperback

This book is part of the Cambridge Primary Maths project. This is an innovative combination of curriculum and resources designed to support teachers and learners to succeed in primary mathematics through best-practice international maths teaching and a problem-solving approach.

To get involved, visit
www.cie.org.uk/cambridgeprimarymaths.

Introduction

This *Skills Builder activity book* is part of a series of 12 write-in activity books for primary mathematics grades 1–6. It can be used as a standalone book, but the content also complements *Cambridge Primary Maths*. Learners progress at different rates, so this series provides a Skills Builder and a Challenge Activity Book for each Primary Mathematics Curriculum Framework Stage to support and broaden the depth of learning.

The *Skills Builder* books consolidate the learning already covered in the classroom, but provide extra support by giving short reminders of key information, topic vocabulary and hints on how best to develop maths skills and knowledge. They have also been written to support learners whose first language is not English.

How to use the books

The activities are for use by learners in school or at home, with adult mediation. Topics have been carefully chosen to focus on those common areas where learners might need extra support. The approach is linked directly to *Cambridge Primary Maths*, but teachers and parents can pick and choose which activities to cover, or go through the books in sequence.

The varied set of activities grow in challenge through each unit, including:

- closed questions with answers, so progress can be checked
- questions with more than one possible answer
- activities requiring resources, for example, dice, spinners or digit cards
- activities and games best done with someone else, for example, in class or at home, which give the opportunity to be fully involved in the child's learning
- activities to support different learning styles: working individually, in pairs, in groups.

How to approach the activities

Space is provided for learners to write their answers in the book. Some activities might need further practice or writing, so students could be given a blank notebook at the start of the year to use alongside the book. Each activity follows a standard structure.

- **Remember** gives an overview of key learning points. They introduce core concepts and, later, can be used as a revision guide. These sections should be read with an adult who can check understanding before attempting the activities.
- **Vocabulary** assists with difficult mathematical terms, particularly when English is not the learner's first language. Learners should read through the key vocabulary with an adult and be encouraged to clarify understanding.

- **Hints** prompt and assist in building understanding, and steer the learner in the right direction.
- **You will need** gives learners, teachers and parents a list of resources for each activity.
- **Photocopiable resources** are provided at the end of the book, for easy assembly in class or at home.
- **Links** to the Cambridge International Examinations Primary Mathematics Curriculum Framework objectives and the corresponding *Cambridge Primary Mathematics Teacher's Resource* are given in the footnote on every page.
- **Calculators** should be used to help learners understand numbers and the number system, including place value and properties of numbers. However, the calculator is not promoted as a calculation tool before Stage 5.

Note:

When a 'spinner' is included, put a paperclip flat on the page so the end is over the centre of the spinner. Place the pencil point in the centre of the spinner, through the paperclip. Hold the pencil firmly and spin the paperclip to generate a result.

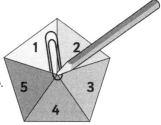

Tracking progress

Answers to closed questions are given at the back of the book; these allow teachers, parents and learners to check their work.

When completing each activity, teachers and parents are advised to encourage self-assessment by asking the students how straightforward they found the activity. When learners are reflecting on games, they should consider how challenging the mathematics was, not who won. Learners could use a ✓/ ✗ or red/green colouring system to record their self-assessment anywhere on each activity page.

These assessments provide teachers and parents with an understanding of how best to support individual learners' next steps.

Working in the 100 square

Remember

A 100 square helps you to count in ones along each row, backwards and forwards, and in tens going up and down each column.

You will need: red and blue counters

Vocabulary

ones, tens, row, column, count, pattern

1	2	3	4	5	6	7	8	9	10
11	12	13	14	15	16	17	18	19	20
21	22	23	24	25	26	27	28	29	30
31	32	33	34	35	36	37	38	39	40
41	42	43	44	45	46	47	48	49	50
51	52	53	54	55	56	57	58	59	60
61	62	63	64	65	66	67	68	69	70
71	72	73	74	75	76	77	78	79	80
81	82	83	84	85	86	87	88	89	90
91	92	93	94	95	96	97	98	99	100

Counting on in ones

Counting on in tens

Unit 1A Number and problem solving
CPM Framework 2Nn1, 2Nn3, 2Nn6, 2Nn7, 2Pt3; CPM Teacher's Resource 1.1

Example

Put two red counters on number 4. Count on five squares, following the arrows across the row. Move one of the counters to the new number.

Put two blue counters on 4, on top of the red one. Count down the column five squares, following the arrows down the column. Move one of the blue counters to the new number.

I counted in | (ones) tens | from 4 to 9. I counted in | ones (tens) | from 4 to 54.

Use the red and blue counters again. Start on 2. Count across six squares. Start at 2 again. Count down the column 6 squares.

Complete these sentences to show what you did.

I counted in | ones tens | from 2 to [   ] .

I counted in | ones tens | from 2 to [   ] .

Now choose your own start numbers and how many jumps to make.

Complete these sentences to show what you did.

I counted in | ones tens | from [   ] to [   ] .

I counted in | ones tens | from [   ] to [   ] .

When you count in rows you always count in | ones tens | .

When you count up and down a column you always count in | ones tens | .

Hint: As you count, move the counter one space.

Number pairs to 10

Remember
When you are thinking about number bonds or pairs to 10, it doesn't matter which order you write the numbers, they are the same pair.

Vocabulary
number pairs, number bonds

Find all the numbers pairs for 10.

X	1	2	3	4	5	6	7	8	9	X

Cross out each number as you use it. Write each number pair twice in the table, just like 0 and 10. Two have already been done for you.

0 + 10 = 10				
10 + 0 = 10				

Which number could you not use? Write down the number bond for it.

☐ + ☐ = 10

Oh no! Gremlins have been here and taken some numbers.

Write in the pairs that add to 10. Make sure they all look different.

2 + 8 = 10			4 + ☐ = 10	
	3 + ☐ = 10	6 + ☐ = 10		9 + ☐ = 10

Hint: Try reversing the order of the numbers within the pairs to find all the possible pairs.

Unit 1A Number and problem solving
CPM Framework 2Nc1, 2Nc10, 2Nc14, 2Pt3; CPM Teacher's Resource 3.1

Number pairs for 100

Remember

Multiples of 10 have 0 in the ones place. Look at the tens digit to find the value of the number.

Vocabulary

multiples, number pairs, number bonds, equals

Here are the multiples of 10 to 100. Two have already been done for you.

~~X~~	10	20	30	40	50	60	70	80	90	1~~0~~0

Find all the pairs of these numbers that add to 100.

Cross out each number as you use it. Write each number pair twice in the table, just like 0 and 100. Some have already been done for you.

0 + 100 = 100			
100 + 0 = 100			

Which number could you not use? Write down the number bond for it.

☐ + ☐ = 100

Oh no! The gremlins are back!

Write in the pairs that equal 100. Make sure they all look different.

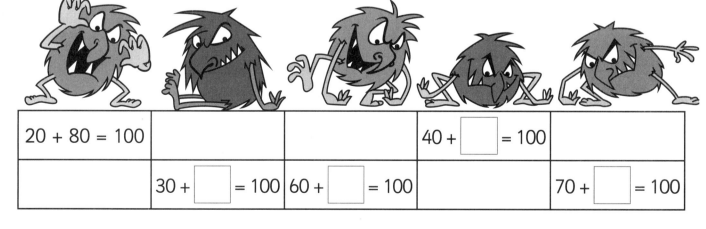

20 + 80 = 100			40 + ☐ = 100	
	30 + ☐ = 100	60 + ☐ = 100		70 + ☐ = 100

Hint: Use what you have found out about number pairs to 10 to help you find number pairs to 100.

Unit 1A Number and problem solving
CPM Framework 2Nn4, 2Nn6, 2Nc1, 2Nc3, 2Nc10, 2Nc14, 2Pt3; CPM Teacher's Resource 3.1

7

Count along the number track

Remember
When counting along a number track, don't count the space you are already in.

You will need: resource 1, page 60, a 1–6 dice or resource 2, page 61, a counter for each player

Vocabulary
number track

Start at 0, count in fives. Colour the numbers.

Start at 0 on the other track. Count in tens. Colour the numbers.

Which numbers are coloured on both tracks?

_____

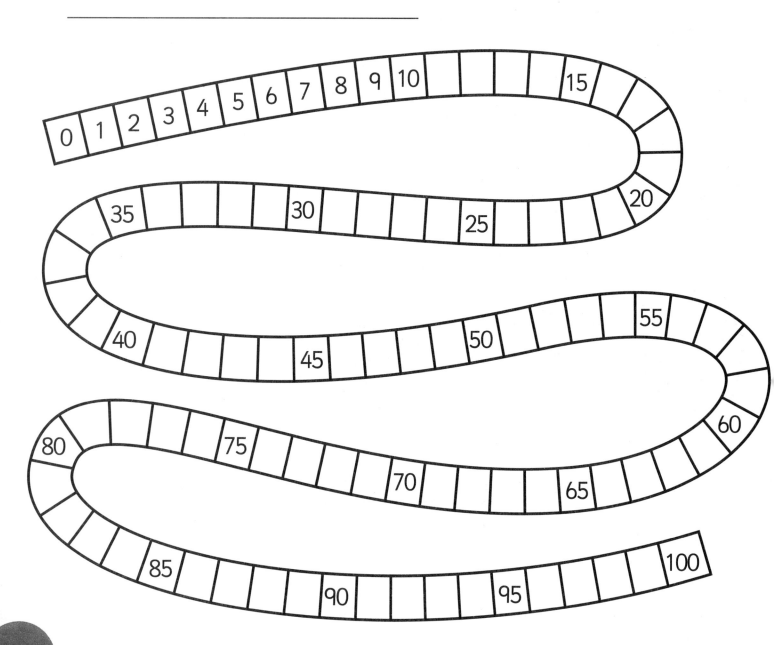

Unit 1A Number and problem solving
CPM Framework 2Nn1, 2Nn3, 2Nn4, 2Nn9, 2Nn10, 2Pt2, 2Pt3, 2Pt8; CPM Teacher's Resource 2.1, 4.1

Now use the tracks as a game for two players.

Decide who will have each track.

Place your counter on 0 on your track. Take turns to throw the dice and move that number of spaces. If there is no number in the space you land on, write the number that is missing.

The first player to reach 100 is the winner.

Play the game several times. Did the same player win each time?

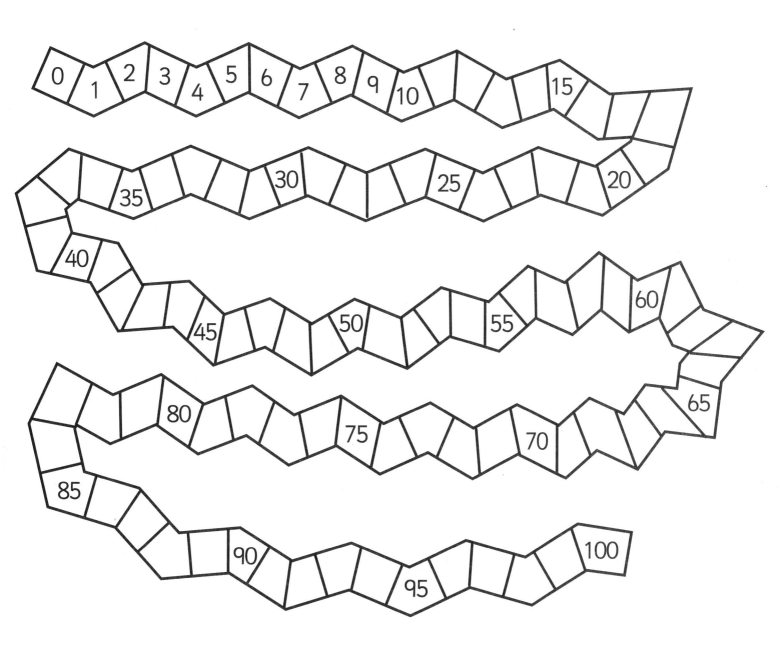

Hint: Use a number line or 100 square for support.

Unit 1A Number and problem solving
CPM Framework 2Nn1, 2Nn3, 2Nn4, 2Nn9, 2Nn10, 2Pt2, 2Pt3, 2Pt8; CPM Teacher's Resource 2.1, 4.1

9

Playing with 20

Remember
When finding pairs to 20, use what you found out when making pairs to 10.

Vocabulary
number pairs, number bonds

Use the first two rows of the 100 square to help you find all the number pairs for 20. The first one is done for you.

1	2	3	4	5	6	7	8	9	10
11	12	13	14	15	16	17	18	19	20

Join the number pairs that make 20, for example 9 and 11.

Write the two number sentences in the table.

The first one is done for you.

$9 + 11 = 20$	$11 + 9 = 20$

There are three more ways to make 20 if you write two more numbers. What are they?

Hint: What if 0 was added to the line? Would that help to find another pair that makes 20?

Unit 1A Number and problem solving
CPM Framework 2Nn1, 2Nc1, 2Nc2, 2Nc14, 2Pt1, 2Pt3; CPM Teacher's Resource 5.1

Adding

Remember

It does not matter in which order you add numbers together, the total will always be the same.

You will need: resource 1, page 60, or a 1–100 number line

Vocabulary
calculation, consecutive numbers, add, +, equals, =

Add each set of four numbers.

You can put the numbers in a different order.

Look for number pairs for 10.

If there are no pairs for 10, think about how you could make a pair for 10.

$1 + 2 + 3 + 4 =$ _____

$2 + 3 + 4 + 5 =$ _____

$3 + 4 + 5 + 6 =$ _____

$4 + 5 + 6 + 7 =$ _____

$5 + 6 + 7 + 8 =$ _____

$6 + 7 + 8 + 9 =$ _____

What do you notice about each total?

Hint: Make pairs for 10 by splitting one of the numbers into two parts and using one of the parts to make 10. Remember to add all the parts of any number, or the total will be incorrect.

Unit 1A Number and problem solving
CPM Framework 2Nn14, 2Nc1, 2Nc8, 2Nc14, 2Pt1, 2Pt3, 2Pt9; CPM Teacher's Resource 6.1

11

Spotty leopard

You will need: a 1–6 dice or resource 2, page 61, a selection of counters (1 for each player and some to cover the spots)

Remember
You can add numbers in any order.

Hint: Use a number line or 100 square to help work out the answers to the calculations.

Vocabulary
add, subtract, calculation

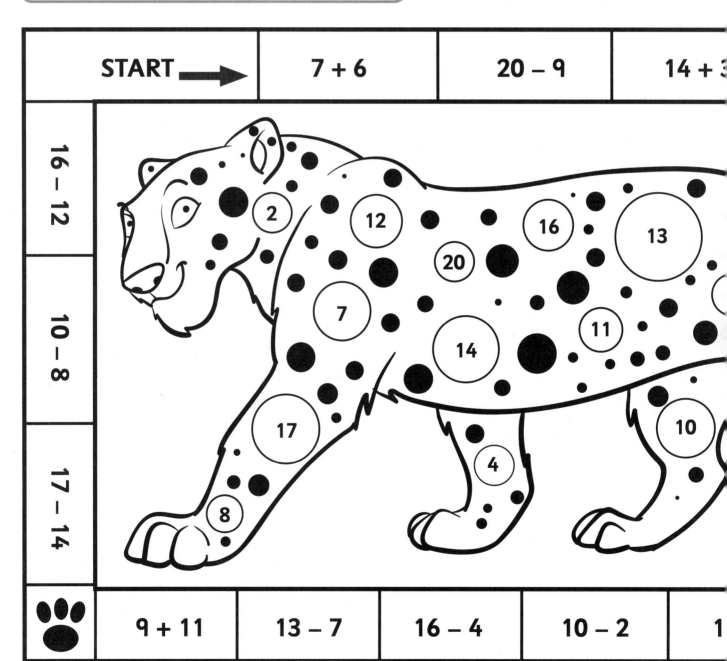

START ➡	7 + 6	20 – 9	14 + 3

16 – 12

10 – 8

17 – 14

	9 + 11	13 – 7	16 – 4	10 – 2	

Numbers on the leopard: 2, 12, 16, 13, 20, 7, 11, 14, 17, 10, 4, 8

Unit 1A Number and problem solving
CPM Framework 2Nc1, 2Nc2, 2Nc11, 2Nc14, 2Nc15, 2Pt1, 2Pt2, 2Pt3; CPM Teacher's Resource 5.2

You can play this game on your own or with a friend. Take turns to throw the dice and move on that number of spaces. Complete each calculation. Put a counter on the spot on the leopard that matches your answer.

Some spots may be the answer to more than one calculation.

If you land on a paw print you can choose any number to cover.

Who will cover the last spot on the leopard?

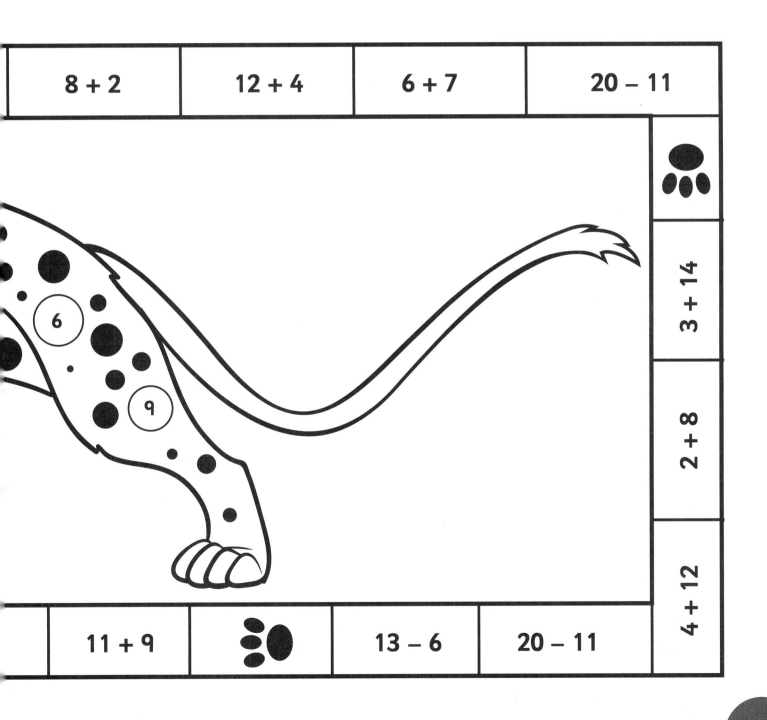

| 8 + 2 | 12 + 4 | 6 + 7 | 20 – 11 |

3 + 14

2 + 8

4 + 12

| 11 + 9 | | 13 – 6 | 20 – 11 |

Unit 1A Number and problem solving
CPM Framework 2Nc1, 2Nc2, 2Nc11, 2Nc14, 2Nc15, 2Pt1, 2Pt2, 2Pt3; CPM Teacher's Resource 5.2

13

Multiplication arrays

You will need: cubes

Remember

An array organises objects into rows and columns to make them easier to count. Counting in twos, three, fours or fives is quicker than counting in ones.

Vocabulary

multiplication, multiply, array

Hint: Use cubes to copy each array. Turn the cube arrays a quarter turn to see the second addition and multiplication.

For each array, write two repeated additions and two multiplication calculations.

The first one is done for you.

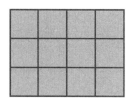

$3 + 3 + 3 + 3 = 12$
$4 + 4 + 4 = 12$
$4 \times 3 = 12$
$3 \times 4 = 12$

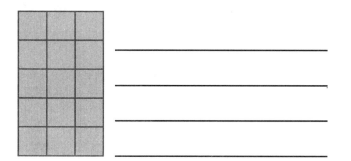

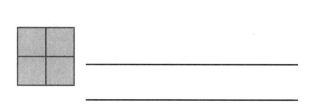

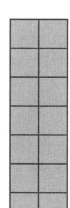

Unit 1A Number and problem solving
CPM Framework 2Nn4, 2Nn5, 2Nc8, 2Nc16, 2Nc17, 2Pt3; CPM Teacher's Resource 7.1

Shapes are everywhere

Remember
Shapes are all around you — at home, at school, in the park, all over the world!

You will need: resource 3, page 62

Vocabulary
shape, circle, square, rectangle, regular pentagon, regular hexagon, triangle, side, corners, vertex

This is a ___circle___ .
It has __1__ side and __0__ corners.

This is a _____ .
It has _____ sides and _____ corners.

This is a _____ .
It has _____ sides and _____ corners.

This is a _____ .
It has _____ sides and _____ corners.

This is a _____ .
It has _____ sides and _____ corners.

This is a _____ .
It has _____ sides and _____ corners.

Complete the sentences in each box. The first one has been done for you.

Look around you. Find one of each of these shapes in the room.

Draw it on the recording sheet and write down where you found it.

Just draw one of each shape.

If there isn't a matching shape, try looking in other rooms or outside.

Talk about the shapes you have found.

3D Shapes

You will need: a tetrahedral dice from resource 2, page 61 and Resource 3, page 62

Remember
3D shapes are solid shapes, not flat. Every flat face on a 3D shape is a 2D shape.

Vocabulary
cone, cuboid, cube, sphere, pyramid, cylinder, symmetry, line of symmetry, face, vertex, vertices

	This is a ___cube___ . It has ___6___ faces and ___8___ vertices.
	This is a _____. It has _____ faces and _____ vertices.
	This is a _____. It has _____ faces and _____ vertices.
	This is a _____. It has _____ faces and _____ vertices.
	This is a _____. It has _____ faces and _____ vertices.
	This is a _____. It has _____ faces and _____ vertices.

Complete the sentences in each box. The first one has been done for you.

Find one of each of these shapes in the room. Draw it on the recording sheet and write where you found it.

If there isn't one, look in other rooms or outside.

Talk about the shapes you have found.

Unit 1B Geometry and problem solving
CPM Framework 2Gs2, 2Gs4; CPM Teacher's Resource 8.2, 8.3

How long is a piece of string?

Remember

When measuring length it is important to measure from the start of the measuring scale

You will need: a piece of string 1 metre long, a pair of scissors, a metre stick, paper for recording

How long is a piece of string?

This is a game for two players.

Vocabulary
measure, length, long, short, metre (m), centimetre (cm), estimate

Player 1 takes the metre length of string and cuts a piece from it.

Both players write down how long they think the first piece of string is now.

I think the string is now 85 cm long.

Use a metre stick to measure the string. Write down the result.

The string is now 82 cm long.

The player whose estimate is closer to the actual length wins 1 point.

Now player 2 cuts a length from the same string.

Repeat the estimating and measuring.

Continue playing until each player has cut the string 3 times.

The winner is the player with more points.

What time is it?

You will need: counters (2 colours), a paperclip and pencil to use the spinner

Remember

The long hand points to 12 for **o'clock** and 6 for **half past.**

This is a game for two players.

Take turns to spin the spinner. Choose a clock with a matching time.

Tell your partner the time on the clock.

If you get the time right, put one of your counters on the clock.

The first person to get four clocks in a line is the winner.

Challenge:

Play the game again. Change the rules. Cover your partner's counter, take off one of their counters or change the rules in some other way.

Hint: Look at the counters already on the gameboard to help decide where to put the next counter.

Unit 1C Measure and problem solving
CPM Framework 2Mt1, 2Mt3, 2Pt2; CPM Teacher's Resource 10.1

Vocabulary

clock, hands, hour, minute, o'clock, half past

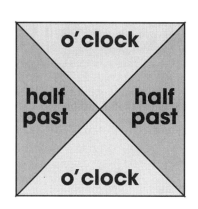

Tens and ones game

Remember
In a two-digit number, the first digit is the number of tens and the second digit is the number of ones.

You will need: digit cards 0–9 cut from resource 5, page 64, counters

Vocabulary
digit, tens, ones, value, closest

This is a game for two players.

Shuffle a set of digit cards and place them in a pile, face down, on the table.

Game 1: Take turns to take two digit cards. Place them on your table below. Once placed, cards cannot be moved. Aim to make a high number. The number that is closest in value to 100 earns a counter.

Repeat. The first player to get five counters is the winner.

Game 2: Play again, aiming to make the lowest number. The number that is closest in value to 1 earns a counter.

Repeat. The first player to get five counters is the winner.

Game 3: Play again but choose a target number between 0 and 100, for example 50.

Repeat. The player that is closest to the target number is the winner.

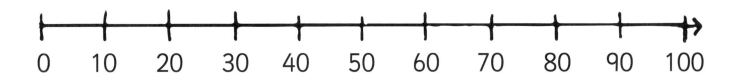

Unit 2A Number and problem solving
CPM Framework 2Nn1, 2Nn6, 2Nn10, 2Nn12, 2Pt2, 2Pt3; CPM Teacher's Resource 12.1

Player 1	
tens	**ones**

Hint: Place high digits in the tens place to make a high number but in the ones space to make a low number. Use a number line to find out which number is closest to 100 or 1.

Player 2	
tens	**ones**

Less than, greater than

Remember

When comparing two-digit numbers, look first at the tens digit to find which number is higher or lower. If they are the same, look at the ones digit.

You will need: resource 1, page 60, digit cards 0–9 cut from resource 5, page 64, a paperclip and pencil to use the spinner

Shuffle the digit cards.

Turn over the top four cards to make two two-digit numbers. Spin the spinner.

Use the numbers and the symbol on the spinner to write a number sentence.

For example:

Vocabulary

digit, tens, ones, two-digit number

is less than

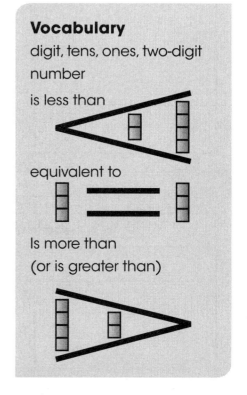

equivalent to

Is more than (or is greater than)

The first number sentence has been done for you.

Write nine more.

23 < 52				

Hint: Use the 100 square (or a number line) to compare the numbers made.

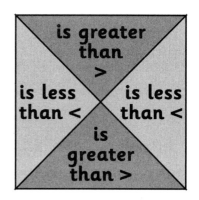

Unit 2A Number and problem solving
CPM Framework 2Nn6, 2Nn12, 2Pt3; CPM Teacher's Resource 12.1, 12.2

Winning hands

Remember
When making a high two-digit number, put a high card in the tens place.

You will need: 1–6 digit cards cut from resource 5, page 64, 12 counters, a paperclip and pencil to use the spinner

Vocabulary
two-digit number, add, subtract

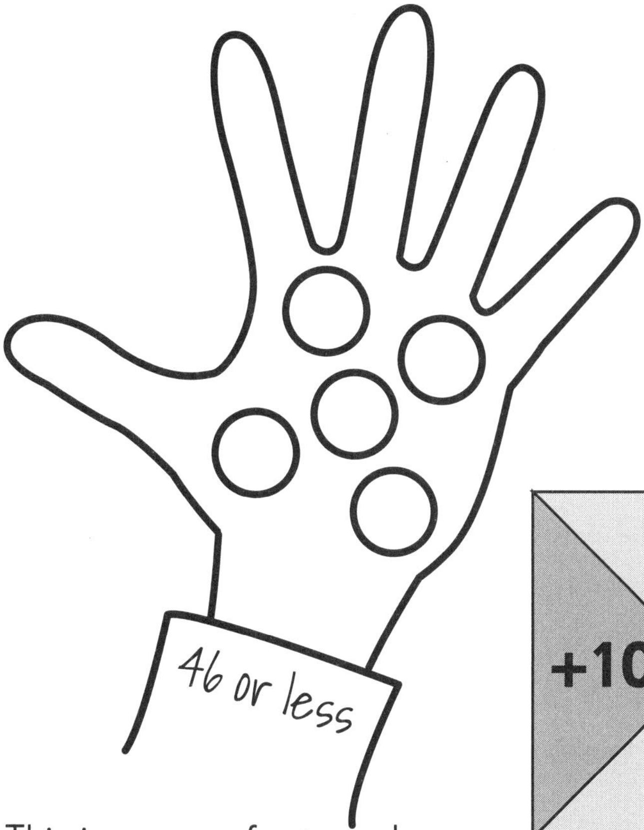

46 or less

−10

+10   +10

−10

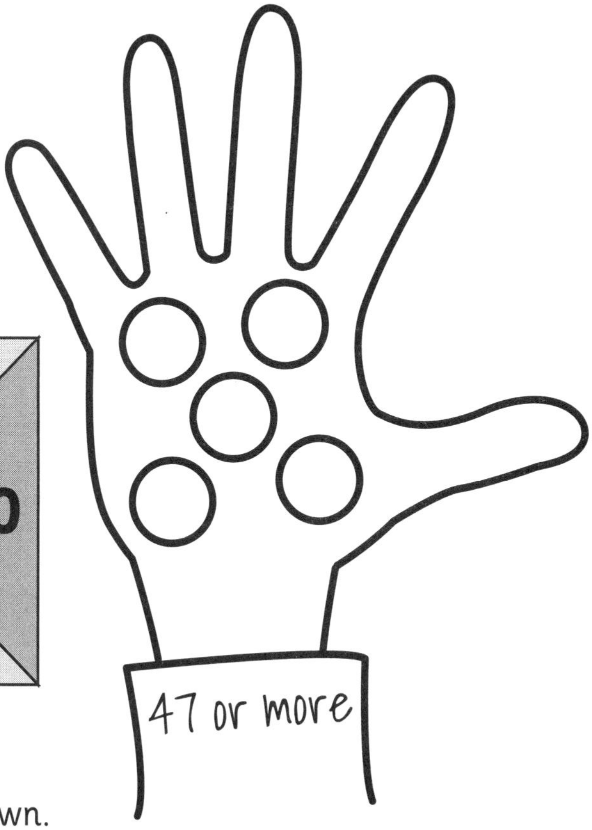

47 or more

This is a game for two players.

Choose one of the hands shown above.

Shuffle the digit cards and spread them out, face down.

Take turns to pick up two cards and make a two-digit number.

Spin the spinner and do the addition or subtraction.

Can the answer go on your hand? If so, put a counter over one of the circles.

Shuffle all the cards and lay them out again.

The first player with a handful of six counters wins.

Hint: Find 46 and 47 on a number line. If the number is to the left of 47 the counter belongs on the left hand. If it is to the right of 46, the counter belongs on the right hand.

Guess and check

You will need: a pack of playing cards with the picture cards removed or 4 sets of 0–9 digit cards from resource 5, page 64

Remember

An estimate is a sensible guess that is close to the right answer. You are not trying to find an exact answer.

Vocabulary

estimate, guess, total, difference

This is a game for two players.

Shuffle the cards and lay them in a pile, face down on the table. Each take a card from the top of the pile and lay it, face down, in front of you.

Guess the number on your card. Then turn your card over and find the difference between your guess and the actual number.

Write in on your score card.

Repeat until you both have both recorded five differences.

Estimate the total of those 'difference' numbers and record your estimate on your score card.

Total your 'difference' numbers. Find the difference between your estimate and your total.

The player with the lower final difference is the winner.

Hint: Use number pairs for 10, doubles, near doubles or any other favourite method to find the totals of the guessed numbers.

Player 1	
Estimate	**Difference**
Total of estimates	**Final difference**

Player 2	
Estimate	**Difference**
Total of estimates	**Final difference**

Unit 2A Number and problem solving
CPM Framework 2Nc8, 2Nc13, 2Nc15; CPM Teacher's Resource 13.1

Number patterns

Remember
Even numbers are multiples of 2. Odd numbers are not multiples of 2. If you sort an odd number of cubes into twos, you will always have 1 cube left over.

Vocabulary
add, odd, even

You will need:
a counter for each loose line, resource 2, page 61

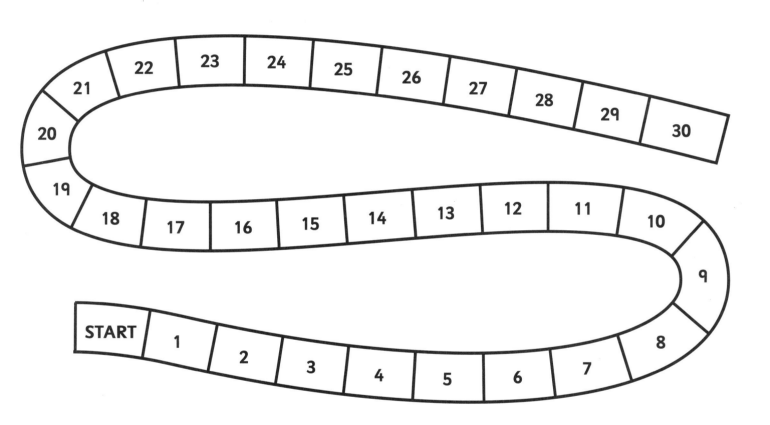

This is a game for two players.

Take turns to roll both dice and add the numbers.

If the total is an odd number, player 1 moves forward that number of squares.

If the total is an even number, player 2 moves forward that number of squares.

Both counters can land on the same square.

The winner is the first person to reach or pass 30.

Sorting numbers

Remember

A Carroll diagram is used to sort numbers or objects according to certain rules.

Vocabulary
Carroll diagram, odd numbers, even numbers

Write each number where it belongs in the Carroll diagram.

Talk to a partner about the numbers if you're not sure.

	Odd numbers	Even numbers
Less than 10	9	
Not less than 10		18

Hint: Start by finding all the odd numbers. Write them in the first column.

Unit 2A Number and problem solving
CPM Framework 2Nn1, 2Nn14, 2Nn15, 2Dh2, 2Pt2; CPM Teacher's Resource 14.3

Using Carroll diagrams

Remember
A Carroll diagram is used to sort numbers or objects according to certain rules.

Vocabulary
Carroll diagram, odd, even, multiple

Choose your own rules for this Carroll diagram.

Write a few numbers in your diagram.

Challenge your partner to complete it.

Check the answers with your friend.

Do they agree with what you would do?

Talk to a partner and explain any changes you would make.

Listen to what your partner has to say.

Hint: Use the numbers to 20 first, then include higher numbers.

Cover a number

You will need: 12 counters in one colour, 12 counters in another colour, two 1–6 dice or resource 2, page 61

Remember

When adding two numbers it may be easier to start with the higher number.

Vocabulary

add, higher, lower

This is a game for two players.

Before you start, decide who will have which grid and which colour counters.

Hint: Players may quickly see that with the original game it is impossible to throw 1. Therefore it would be best not to put a counter in a row that has a 1. Let players find this out for themselves. This may be through discussion with a friend or trial and error.

Player 1					
2	9	1	7	10	4
5	12	3	6	8	11
2	9	1	7	10	4
5	12	3	6	8	11

Unit 2A Number and problem solving
CPM Framework 2Nc8, 2Nc11, 2Nc14, 2Pt1, 2Pt2, 2Pt3; CPM Teacher's Resource 15.1

Take turns to roll both dice.

Add the numbers together.

Put a counter on that number in your grid.

If there is nowhere to put your counter, roll the dice again.

When all of your counters are used up, the game is over.

Each player chooses one column of their grid and adds up any numbers in that column that have a counter on them.

The player with the higher total wins the game.

Make a new game using the same grids.

You could:

1 change the numbers

2 change the dice

3 choose whether to add or subtract each time. It doesn't have to be the same all through the game.

Player 2					
6	3	11	5	10	9
7	12	3	2	8	1
2	4	1	12	5	4
10	7	9	8	6	11

Find the difference

Remember

Find the difference by counting on from the smaller number or counting back from the larger number.

Vocabulary

difference

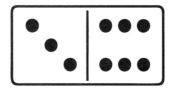

The difference is 3

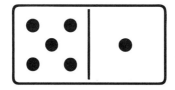

The difference is 4

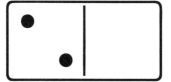

The difference is 2

Place a set of dominoes face down on the table in front of you.

Choose three and turn them over. Draw the spots on these dominoes.

Find the differences.

The difference is ____

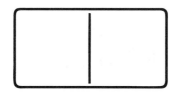

The difference is ____

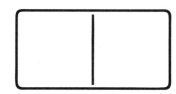

The difference is ____

Choose three more dominoes.

Find the differences.

The difference is ____

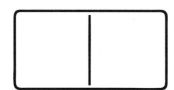

The difference is ____

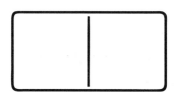

The difference is ____

Unit 2A Number and problem solving
CPM Framework 2Nc13, 2Nc15, 2Pt1; CPM Teacher's Resource 16.1

Find a domino with the given difference. Draw the spots.
Don't use a domino that you have already used.

The difference is 2

The difference is 4

The difference is 1

The difference is 3

The difference is 0

The difference is 5

Now find the difference for each pair of 2 digit numbers.

23 27

The difference is

_____

34 39

The difference is

_____

41 45

The difference is

_____

29 31

The difference is

_____

38 42

The difference is

_____

47 53

The difference is

_____

Hint: Use half the set of dominoes rather than the whole set.
As children grow in confidence, add more.

Arrays

Remember

When you are multiplying two numbers together you can use an array.

Vocabulary
add, multiply, multiplication, repeated addition, array

Player 1

× 2 = ☐

× 5 = ☐

× 10 = ☐

Hint: Count in 2s, 5s or 10s to find the total number of counters or cubes in each array.

Unit 2A Number and problem solving
CPM Framework 2Nn4, 2Nc16, 2NC17, 2Nc19; CPM Teacher's Resource 17.1, 17.2

This is a game for two players.

Shuffle the cards. Put them in a pile, face down on the table in front of you. Take turns to take a card from the top of the pile. Put it in one of your boxes below. Keep playing until all your boxes have a card in them.

Both players make arrays with counters or cubes to work out each calculation. Each player chooses their two highest answers. Add them together. The player with the greater total is the winner.

Play 3 rounds. The player who wins more rounds is the overall winner.

Player 2

× 2 = ☐

× 5 = ☐

× 10 = ☐

Grouping and sharing

Remember

When you are putting objects into groups, each group must have the same amount.

You will need: counters or cubes, a paperclip and pencil to use the spinner

Vocabulary

group, size, divide, division

Spin the tens spinner and collect that number of counters or cubes.

Spin the group spinner to find out what size groups to make.

Put the cubes into the correct group size.

The first one has been done for you.

I started with ___20___ cubes and made groups of _2_ .

There are __10__ groups.

20	÷	2	=	10

I started with _____ cubes and made groups of _____.

There are _____ groups.

☐ ÷ ☐ = ☐

I started with _____ cubes and made groups of _____.

There are _____ groups.

☐ ÷ ☐ = ☐

Group spinner

I started with _____ cubes and made groups of _____.

There are _____ groups.

☐ ÷ ☐ = ☐

I started with _____ cubes and made groups of _____.

There are _____ groups.

☐ ÷ ☐ = ☐

Tens spinner

I started with _____ cubes and made groups of _____.

There are _____ groups.

☐ ÷ ☐ = ☐

I started with _____ cubes and made groups of _____.

There are _____ groups.

☐ ÷ ☐ = ☐

Write what you did and what you found out.

_____

_____

Hint: Before starting the activity, arrange the cubes in sticks of tens. Copy the example first, to see what to do.

Venn diagrams

You will need: 3 counters the same colour for each player, a 1–6 dice and a tetrahedral dice or resource 2, page 61

Remember

Venn diagrams are useful for sorting information. The label for each ring tells you what information belongs within that ring. Information that belongs in both rings goes in the overlap.

Vocabulary
represent, sort, set, Venn diagram, multiplication, repeated addition, array

Venn game 1

This is a game for two players.

Each player needs three counters. Take turns to throw the two dice and multiply the numbers together.

Put one of your counters in the part of the Venn diagram where the answer to your multiplication belongs.

If it doesn't belong in either of the circles, or you already have a counter there, miss that turn.

You cannot place more than one of your counters in any of the sections.

The game ends when one player has a counter in every section.

You could play the game again, using six or nine counters each.

Put two or three in each section.

Venn game 2

Play again with six counters each. Put two counters in each section.

Think of some ideas for your own Venn diagram game.

You can use dice, a spinner or something else.

Play your game with a partner.

Choose how to record what you found out.

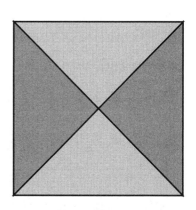

Hint: Use repeated addition or an array to find the answer to the multiplication.

Unit 2B Handling data
CPM Framework 2Nn4, 2Nn5, 2Nn14, 2Nn15, 2Nc16, 2Nc17, 2Dh2, 2Pt2, 2Pt3, 2Pt4; CPM Teacher's Resource 18.3

Venn game 1

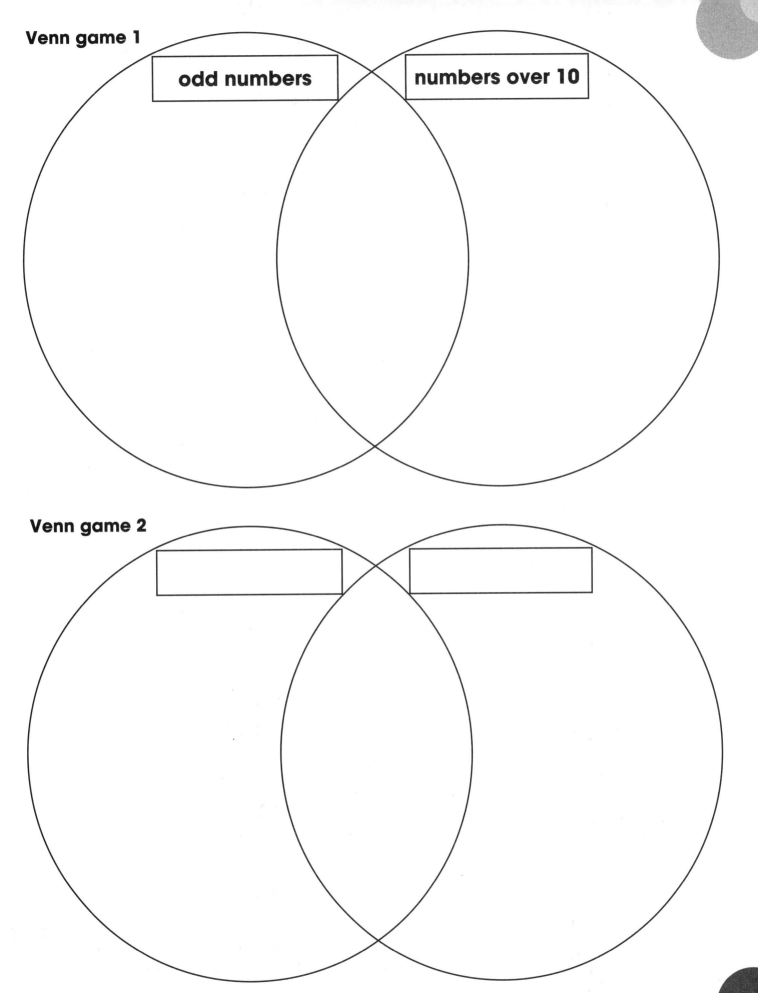

odd numbers

numbers over 10

Venn game 2

CPM Framework 2Nn4, 2Nn5, 2Nn14, 2Nn15, 2Nc16, 2Nc17, 2Dh2, 2Pt2, 2Pt3, 2Pt4; CPM Teacher's Resource 18.3

Make a triangle

Remember

Line up one end of the object to the start of the measuring scale on the ruler. Tessellating patterns are made of shapes that are put together in a pattern with no gaps.

You will need: A4 paper, scissors, tape measure or ruler, spare coloured paper

21cm

A4 paper | 30cm

Vocabulary
length, long, centimetres, wide, half, tessellate

1 Fold the paper in half long-ways, then open it out flat.

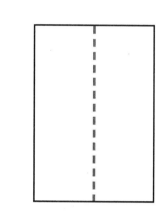

2 Fold a bottom corner up to touch the fold line, making a sharp point on the other corner.

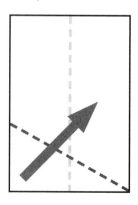

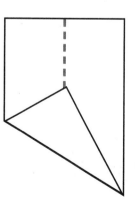

> **Hint**: Use paper of different colours. Cut the A4 paper in half and half again to make rectangles of different sizes.

3 Now fold these two edges together and crease along the new dotted line.

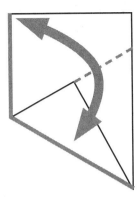 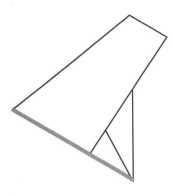

4 Fold the corner over and tuck it under. Turn over to the smooth side.

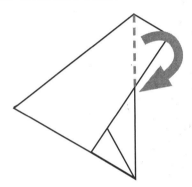 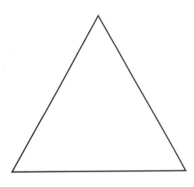

Each side of the triangle measures _____ cm.

Use A6-sized paper.

Make it into a triangle, as before.

Each side of the triangle measures _____ cm.

Make three more small triangles.

Place them on top of your big triangle. What do you notice?

I can use _____ small triangles to make a big triangle.

10.5cm

A6 paper	15cm

Use the triangles to make tessellating patterns.

At the zoo

You will need: 1–6 dice or resource 2, page 61, a counter each (not blue or red) to move around the board, a set of counters to represent litres: blue for 1 litre, red for 10 litres

Remember

Adding measures is the same as adding numbers.

Vocabulary
litre, litres

This is a game for two players.

Each blue counter represents 1 litre.

Each red counter represents 10 litres.

Put your playing counters on **START**.

Take turns to throw the dice and move that number of spaces.

When you land on a litres space, collect the matching amount in counters.

Use the counters to give one or more of the animals some water.

The player who puts the last counter on an animal claims all of those counters. That animal has now had its water for the day and no more can be given to it.

The game ends when all of the animals have been given enough water for a day.

Each player then totals the number of litres they have collected.

The winner is the player with more litres.

Unit 2C Length, height and capacity
CPM Framework 2Nn3, 2Nn4, 2Ml1, 2Ml2, 2Pt2; CPM Teacher's Resource 20.1, 20.2

START
20 litres
100 litres
2 litres
20 litres
10 litres
2 litres
10 litres
20 litres
100 litres
20 litres
10 litres
2 litres
100 litres
2 litres
10 litres
100 litres
20 litres
100 litres
100 litres
2 litres

Closest to 1000g

Remember

We measure weight in grams (g) and kilograms (kg).
1000 grams (g) = 1 kilogram (kg).

You will need: resource 7, page 66

Vocabulary
gram, kilogram, weight, mass, prediction, multiple

This is an activity for two people.

The aim is to get as close to 1000g as possible.

Put the weight cards, face down, in a pile. Take turns to take a card. Draw the arrow on the scales to the position written on the card.

Take a second card.

Draw an arrow to show the combined weight on both cards.

When your scales are showing a weight close to 1000g, you can choose to take another card or 'stick'. You are out if you choose another card and it goes over 1000g.

The player whose scales show a weight closest to 1000g is the winner.

Another game

Start with 1000g.

Take a weight card and subtract this from 1000g.

The player whose scales show the weight closest to 0 is the winner.

Unit 2C Length, height and capacity
CPM Framework 2Ml2, 2Pt1, 2Pt2, 2Pt3; CPM Teacher's Resource 21.1

Player 1

I used:

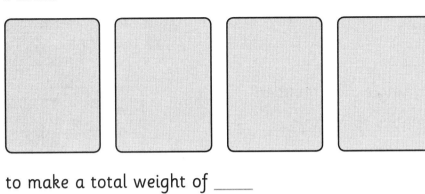

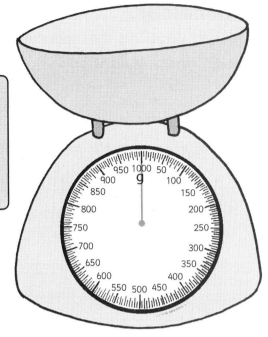

to make a total weight of _____

Player 2

I used:

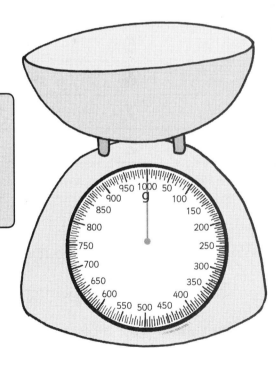

to make a total weight of _____

Doubling doubles

Remember
When doubling a number you add the number to itself or multiply it by 2.

Vocabulary
double, number, digit, odd, even, tens

Complete the table for doubling single-digit numbers.

Use the doubles in a set of dominoes to help you.

How will you find double 7, 8 and 9?

Single-digit number	Double the single-digit number	Odd or even?
1	2	even
2	4	even
3		
4		
5		
6		
7		
8		
9		

What do you notice about all of the answers? _____.

When I double a single-digit number, the answer is always _____.

What about a 2-digit number? Will that always be true? _____.

Try double 10, double 11 and double 15.

When I double a 2-digit number the answer is always _____.

Now try doubling multiples of 5.

Make a prediction.

Put a ring round your prediction.

I think when I double multiples of 5 the answers will be:

odd   even   both odd and even.

Now find out. Complete the table below.

Multiple of 5	Double the multiple of 5	How many tens?
5	10	1
10	20	2
15		
20		
25		
30		
35		
40		
45		
50		

When I double a multiple of 5 the answers are always _____.

When I double the next multiple of 5 the tens increase by _____.

> **Hint**: Use a 100 square to remind you about the pattern of odd and even numbers.

CPM Framework 2Nn1, 2Nn6, 2Nn14, 2Nc11, 2Nc20, 2Nc21, 2Pt1, 2Pt3, 2Pt4, 2Pt8, 2Pt9; CPM Teacher's Resource 22.1

Threes and fours

You will need:
interlocking cubes or counters of three different colours

Remember
Ordinal numbers (1st, 2nd, 3rd, 4th...) are in the same order as counting numbers.

Vocabulary
count, first, second, third, fourth,... 1st, 2nd, 3rd, 4th,...

Vicki and Oliver were getting ready for their party.

They made 20 cakes.

Vicki wanted to put icing on them.

Oliver wanted cherries and sprinkles on his.

They lined up all the cakes.

Vicki put icing on every second cake.

Oliver put a cherry on every third cake and sprinkles on every fourth cake.

There was nothing on the first cake.

Use the first grid to help you find out how each cake is decorated.

Put a yellow cube on cakes with just icing.

Put a red cube on cakes that have a cherry.

Put a blue cube on cakes that have sprinkles.

> **Hint**: To find the number of cakes of each type, count along the grid.

Unit 3A Number and problem solving
CPM Framework 2Nn4, 2Nn5, 2Nn11, 2Pt3, 2Pt4, 2Pt8; CPM Teacher's Resource 23.1, 23.2

1	2	3	4	5	6	7	8	9	10
11	12	13	14	15	16	17	18	19	20

Which cake numbers have no decoration? _____

Which cake numbers had cherries? _____

Which cake numbers had sprinkles? _____

Which cake numbers had only icing? _____

For their next party, they made 50 cakes.
Use this grid to show the pattern of the cakes up to 50.

1	2	3	4	5	6	7	8	9	10
11	12	13	14	15	16	17	18	19	20
21	22	23	24	25	26	27	28	29	30
31	32	33	34	35	36	37	38	39	40
41	42	43	44	45	46	47	48	49	50

Unit 3A Number and problem solving
CPM Framework 2Nn4, 2Nn5, 2Nn11, 2Pt3, 2Pt4, 2Pt8; CPM Teacher's Resource 23.1, 23.2

47

Going to the zoo

You will need: resource 1, page 60, a 1–6 dice and a coin dice from resource 2, page 61, a pile of coins including multiples of cents and dollars, a counter for each player

Remember
There are 100 cents in every dollar.

This is a game for two players.

Each player takes 10 turns to throw the money dice and collect that amount of money.

I have ____ to spend altogether.

Now take turns to roll the 1–6 dice.

Follow the path round the zoo, spending your money as you go.

Keep a running total of what you spend and how much you have left.

Use the 100 square to help you count back.

Vocabulary
money, cents, dollar, spend

Player 1			Player 2		
I have	I spent	What I have left	I have	I spent	What I have left

Unit 3A Number and problem solving
CPM Framework 2Nc11, 2Nc12, 2Nc13, 2Mm1, 2Mm2, 2Mm3, 2Pt3, 2Pt4; CPM Teacher's Resource 24.3, 31.2, 32.2

How much money do you have left when you reach the exit?

Player 1 has _____ .

Player 2 has _____ .

Who has more? _____ .

> **Hint**: After playing the game with dollars and cents, play again using local currency. Amend the prices if necessary. The amount left after each purchase is the amount available to spend next time.

Dividing game

You will need: resource 5, page 64

Remember
When you are dividing, each group must have the same amount. Dividing by 2 is the same as finding a half.

Vocabulary
digit, divide, ÷, solution, equally, total

Hint: Use a number line to help with division, by counting back in equal steps (repeated subtraction).

Player 1	
	0
	0
	0

$\div 2 = \boxed{}$

$\div 5 = \boxed{}$

$\div 10 = \boxed{}$

Unit **3A** Number and problem solving
CPM Framework 2Nn4, 2Nc4, 2Nc18, 2Nc19, 2Pt1, 2Pt2, 2Pt3, 2Pt4, 2Pt8; CPM Teacher's Resource 26.1, 26.3

This is a game for two players.

Shuffle the cards and place them face down in a pile. Take turns to pick up a card. Put it in one of your boxes to make a decade number (multiple of 10). Carry on until all of your boxes have a card in them.

Work out your three divisions.

You could group counters or count in twos, threes, fives or tens to find the solution.

Pick the two divisions that give the lowest answers. Add those two answers.

The person with the lower total wins the game.

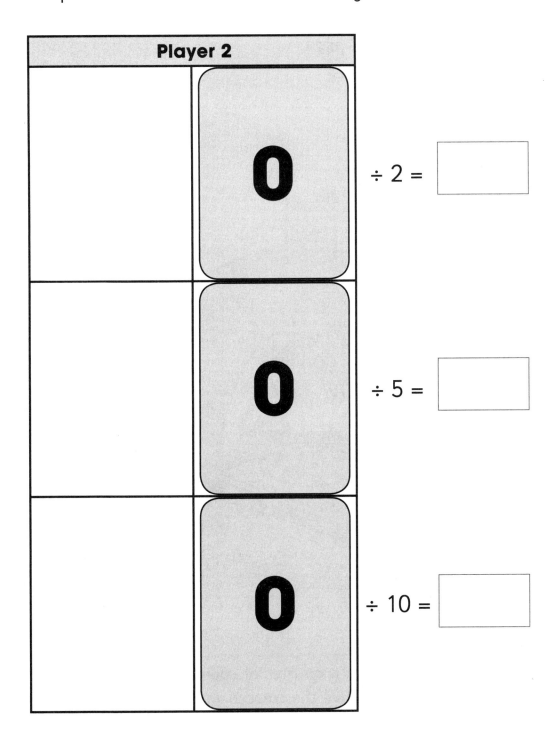

Player 2

0 ÷ 2 = ☐

0 ÷ 5 = ☐

0 ÷ 10 = ☐

CPM Framework 2Nn4, 2Nc4, 2Nc18, 2Nc19, 2Pt1, 2Pt2, 2Pt3, 2Pt4, 2Pt8; CPM Teacher's Resource 26.1, 26.3

Pizza pie

Vocabulary

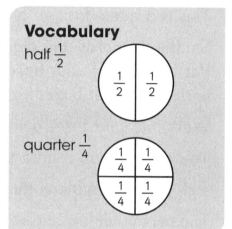

half $\frac{1}{2}$

quarter $\frac{1}{4}$

Remember

When dividing objects into fractions each piece must be equal in size, shape or quantity.

Louis the chef loves to make pizza.

He has to make pizza for two customers.

The first customer wants everything on her pizza.

Share all the toppings shown equally between both halves.

Draw the toppings on the pizza.

The second customer customer also wants everything on his pizza.

Share all the toppings shown equally between the four quarters.

Draw the toppings on the pizza.

Hint: Use cubes or, counters to find half or a quarter of each topping. Place cubes on each slice of pizza to make sure they have the correct amounts of toppings.

Unit 3A Number and problem solving
CPM Framework 2Nn16, 2Nn17, 2Nn19, 2Pt3; CPM Teacher's Resource 25.1, 25.2

Tomatoes

Mushrooms

Anchovies

Salami

Olives

Cheese

Making squares

You will need: resource 8, page 67, scissors, a ruler

Remember

A tangram is a set of shapes that can be fitted together to make a square, and taken apart to make different shapes.

Vocabulary
tangram, shape, triangle, square, quadrilateral

Cut the tangram on the resource sheet along the lines to make seven different shapes.

Take out the square.

Use the other pieces to make as many different squares as you can.

This one is made with four pieces.

You can use two, three, four, five or all six pieces.

Have a go!

Not all of your squares will be the same size.

How many different ways can you find to make a square?

Use the table to record how you made your square.

Draw and name the shapes you make.

Hint: Turn the shapes to fit them together to make a square.

small triangle

small triangle

medium triangle

large triangle

Unit 3B Geometry and problem solving
CPM Framework 2Dh1, 2Gs1, 2Pt3, 2Pt9; CPM Teacher's Resource 28.2

Number of shapes I used	The name of the shapes I used
2 shapes	
3 shapes	
4 shapes	4 triangles
5 shapes	
6 shapes	

Moving the square

You will need: 6 squares from resource 9, page 68, scissors, glue stick

Remember

Turns can be clockwise or anticlockwise

Vocabulary
whole, half, quarter, turn, clockwise, anticlockwise

half turn

quarter turn

Use one square at a time.

Cut off the triangle. Fit the two pieces together, edge to edge, to make a new shape. Here is an example:

How many different shapes can you make?

Glue them onto this page when you have made them.

Hint: Watch out for shapes that are really the same but just turned round or flipped over.

Unit 3B Geometry and problem solving
CPM Framework 2Gs1, 2Gp2, 2Pt2, 2Pt9; CPM Teacher's Resource 29.1, 29.2

Choose a shape

You will need: resource 11, page 69

Remember
Count the sides and corners to remind you of the name of the shape.

Vocabulary
shape, regular, square, rectangle, circle, five-pointed star, symmetrical

This is an activity for two people.

Cut the 2D shapes from resource 11, and spread them out between you.

Player 1 chooses a shape – but does not touch it or say what it is.

Player 2 asks questions to see if they can find the shape.

If they point to it and they are right, they pick it up and players change roles.

If they are wrong, player 1 picks up the shape. Player 1 chooses a new shape for player 2 to ask questions about.

Hint: Talk about which questions were helpful and which were not so helpful. Keep a note of how many questions were needed and try to reduce the number in another game.

Passing time

You will need: 1–9 digit cards from resource 5, page 64, resource 10, page 68

Remember

Analogue and digital clocks can tell the same time, but they look different. Analogue clocks use hands. Digital clocks use numbers.

Vocabulary
time, minutes, hour, analogue, digital

This is a game for two players.

The aim of the game is to make a digital time that is as close as possible to the time on the time card.

Shuffle the digit cards and place them in a pile, face down, on the table.

Take turns to take a digit card and place it into a section on your game board. Once you have placed a number, you cannot move it. Turn over the top time card.

Player 1			

Player 2			

Hint: Use a clock to help decide which time is closer to the time on the time card.

When you have placed three cards, decide whether you want to take a fourth card.

The winner is the player who makes a time that is closest to the time on the time card.

Play the game five times. The player who wins more rounds is the winner.

Unit 3B Geometry and problem solving
CPM Framework 2Nn1, 2Mt1, 2Mt2, 2Mt3, 2Pt2, 2Pt3; CPM Teacher's Resource 32.1

Money, money, money

Remember

Adding coins is the same as adding numbers.

You will need: a selection of coins – one 50c coin, four 25c coins and seven 10c coins for each player

This is a game for two players.

Decide who will go first. Then take turns to put 1 coin on 1 of the squares.

The winner is the first to make a row (horizontally, vertically or diagonally) of coins that add to one dollar. There need not be a coin in every square in the row.

Play again. Do you think it is better to go first or second?

Find some good ways to try to win the game.

Vocabulary

money, coin, cent, dollar

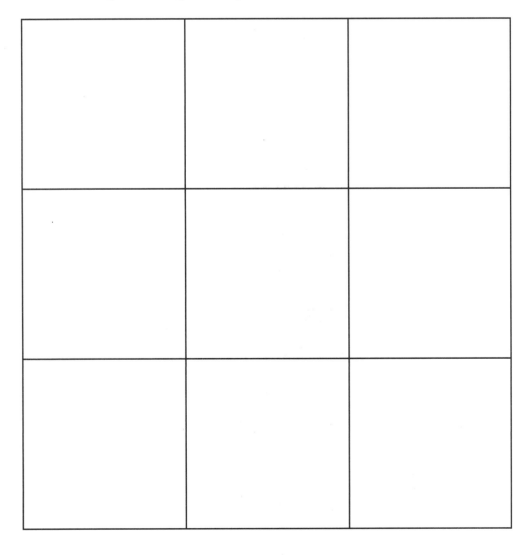

Hint: After using dollars and cents, play again using local currency. Change the target amount if necessary.

Unit 3B Geometry and problem solving
CPM Framework 2Nn1, 2Nc11, 2Nc12, 2Mm1, 2Mm3, 2Pt2; CPM Teacher's Resource 31.2, 32.3

59

Resource 1 100 square

1	2	3	4	5	6	7	8	9	10
11	12	13	14	15	16	17	18	19	20
21	22	23	24	25	26	27	28	29	30
31	32	33	34	35	36	37	38	39	40
41	42	43	44	45	46	47	48	49	50
51	52	53	54	55	56	57	58	59	60
61	62	63	64	65	66	67	68	69	70
71	72	73	74	75	76	77	78	79	80
81	82	83	84	85	86	87	88	89	90
91	92	93	94	95	96	97	98	99	100

Resource 2 Dice templates

Cut out the nets, taking care not to cut off the tabs. Fold along all the lines to make cubes or a pyramid. Tuck the tabs inside and glue them in place, to hold the dice together.

3D shape dice

1–6 Dice

Coin dice

Tetrahedral dice

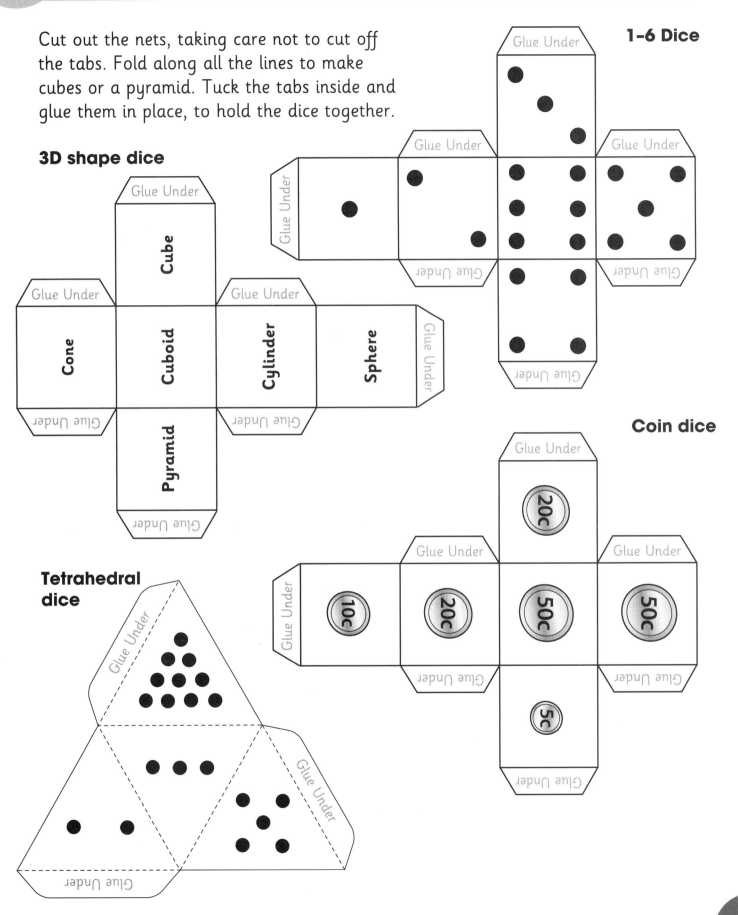

Resource 3 Recording sheet

	This is a I found it
	This is a I found it
	This is a I found it
	This is a I found it
	This is a I found it
	This is a I found it

House

Cat

Car

Tree

Box

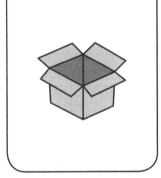

Robot

Tractor

Spider

Table

Chair

Giant

Aeroplane

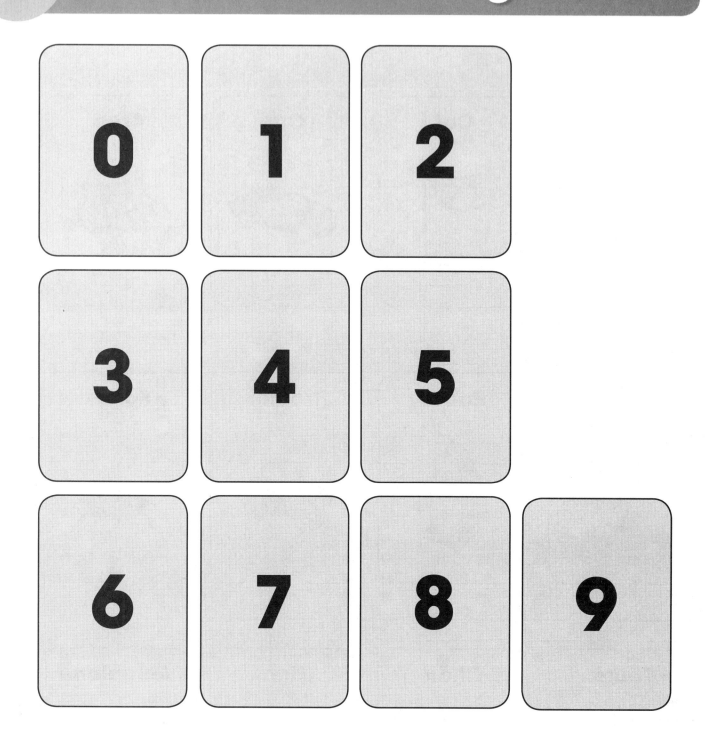

Photocopiable resources

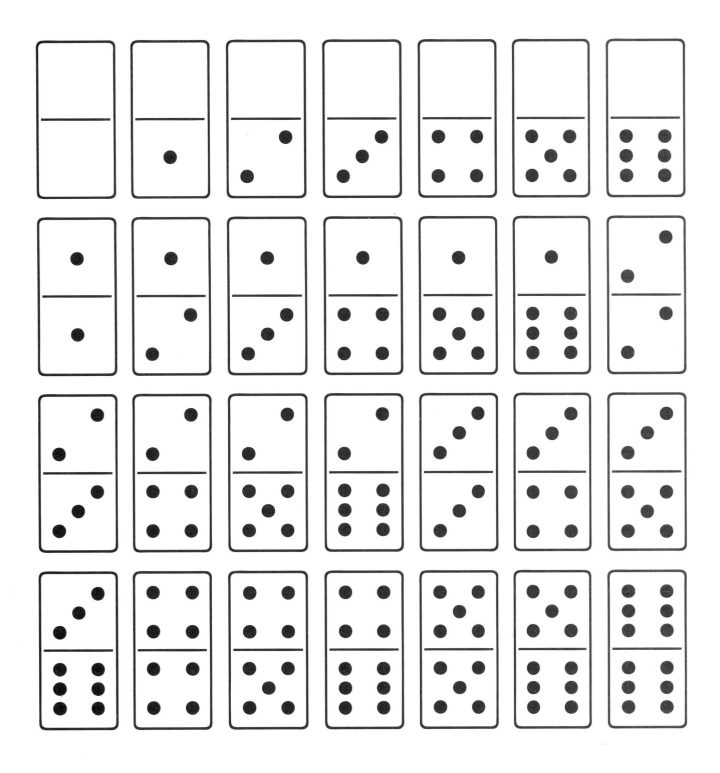

500 g	500 g	250 g	250 g	200 g
200 g	200 g	200 g	200 g	200 g
100 g	100 g	100 g	100 g	100 g
100 g	50 g	50 g	50 g	50 g

Photocopiable resources

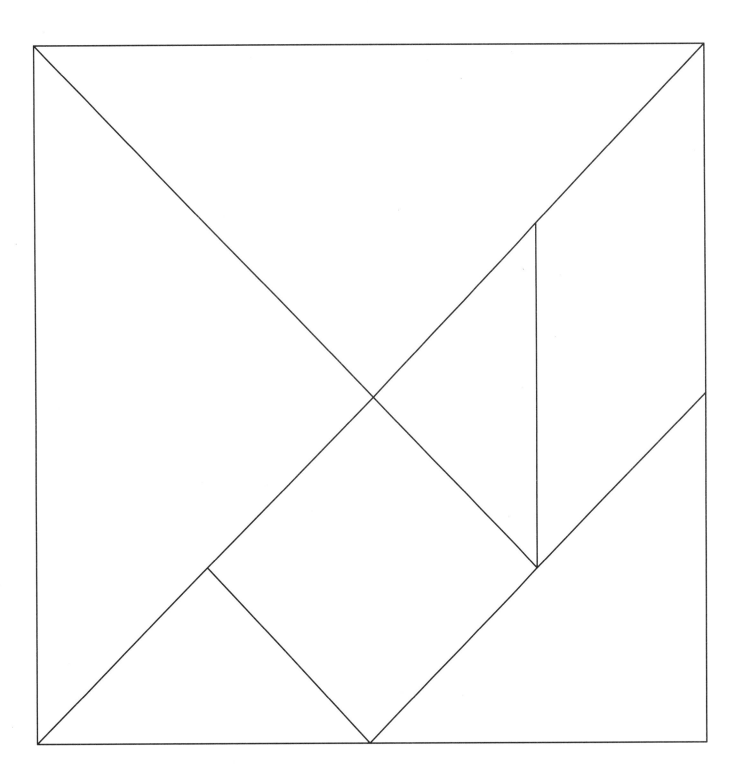

Resource 9 Squares

Resource 10 Time cards

Photocopiable resources

Original material © Cambridge University Press 2016

Resource 11 2D shape cards

Answers

Page 5 Working in the 100 square
$2 + 6 = 8$; $2 + 60 = 62$.
I counted in ones from 2 to 8.
I counted in tens from 2 to 62.

Page 6 Number pairs to 10
$0 + 10$; $1 + 9$; $2 + 8$; $3 + 7$; $4 + 6$; $10 + 0$; $9 + 1$;
$8 + 2$; $7 + 3$; $6 + 4$. Unused number 5, $5 + 5 = 10$.

Page 7 Number pairs for 100
$0 + 100 = 100$, $10 + 90 = 100$, $20 + 80 = 100$,
$30 + 70 = 100$, $40 + 60 = 100$, $100 + 0 = 100$,
$90 + 10 = 100$, $80 + 20 = 100$, $70 + 30 = 100$,
$60 + 40 = 100$. Unused number 50. $50 + 50 = 100$.

Pages 8–9 Counting along the number track
10, 20, 30, 40, 50, 60, 70, 80, 90, 100

Page 10 Playing with 20

$1 + 19 = 20$	$19 + 1 = 20$
$2 + 18 = 20$	$18 + 2 = 20$
$3 + 17 = 20$	$17 + 3 = 20$
$4 + 16 = 20$	$16 + 4 = 20$
$5 + 15 = 20$	$15 + 5 = 20$
$6 + 14 = 20$	$14 + 6 = 20$
$7 + 13 = 20$	$13 + 7 = 20$
$8 + 12 = 20$	$12 + 8 = 20$
$9 + 11 = 20$	$11 + 9 = 20$

Extra numbers are zero and 10

Page 11 Adding
All totals are even numbers. When two numbers are odd, odd + odd = even. When two numbers are even, even + even = even., so the total will also be even. The total on the next line increases by 4, because each of the four numbers has increased by 1.

Page 14 Multiplication arrays
$5 + 5 + 5 = 15$
$3 + 3 + 3 + 3 + 3 = 15$
$3 \times 5 = 15$
$5 \times 3 = 15$

$7 + 7 = 14$
$2 + 2 + 2 + 2 + 2 + 2 + 2 = 14$
$2 \times 7 = 14$
$7 \times 2 = 14$

$1 + 1 + 1 = 3$
$1 \times 3 = 3$
$3 \times 1 = 3$

$2 + 2 + 2 = 6$
$3 + 3 = 6$
$3 \times 2 = 6$
$2 \times 3 = 6$

$2 + 2 = 4$
$2 \times 2 = 4$

Page 15 Shapes are everywhere
This is a triangle. It has 3 sides and 3 corners.
This is a square. It has 4 sides and 4 corners.
This is a rectangle. It has 4 sides and 4 corners.
This is a pentagon. It has 5 sides and 5 corners.
This is a hexagon. It has 6 sides and 6 corners.

Page 16 3D shapes
This is a cuboid. It has 6 faces and 8 vertices.
This is a sphere. It has 1 face and 0 vertices.
This is a cylinder. It has 3 faces and 0 vertices.
This is a cone. It has 2 faces and 1 vertex.
This is a square based pyramid. It has 5 faces and 5 vertices.

Page 26 Sorting numbers

	Odd numbers	Even numbers
Less than 10	1 3 5 7 9	2 4 6 8
Not less than 10	11 13 15 17 19	10 12 14 16 18 20

Page 30 Find the difference
$27 - 23 = 4$, $39 - 34 = 5$, $45 - 41 = 4$,
$31 - 29 = 2$, $42 - 38 = 4$, $53 - 47 = 6$

Page 38 Make a triangle
Each side of the A4 triangle should be 24 cm long.
Each side of the A6 triangle should be 12 cm long.
4 small triangles make a big triangle.

Pages 44–45 Doubling doubles

Single-digit number	Double the single-digit number	Odd or even?
1	2	even
2	4	even
3	6	even
4	8	even
5	10	even
6	12	even
7	14	even
8	16	even
9	18	even

Multiple of 5	Double the multiple of 5	How many tens?
5	10	1
10	20	2
15	30	3
20	40	4
25	50	5
30	60	6
35	70	7
40	80	8
45	90	9
50	100	10

When I double a single-digit number, the answer is always **even**.

When I double a 2-digit number the answer is always **even**.

When I double a multiple of 5 the answers are always **even**.

When I double the next multiple of 5 the tens increase by **one**.

Pages 46–47 Threes and fours

none 1	icing 2	cherry 3	icing, sprinkles 4	none 5	icing, cherry 6	none 7	icing, sprinkles 8	cherry 9	icing 10
none 11	icing, cherry, sprinkles 12	none 13	icing 14	cherry 15	icing, sprinkles 16	none 17	icing 18	none 19	icing, sprinkles 20

Which cake numbers have no decoration? 1, 5, 7, 11, 13, 17, 19

Which cake numbers had cherries? 3, 6, 9, 12, 15, 18

Which cake numbers had sprinkles? 4, 8, 12, 16, 20

Which cake numbers had only icing? 2, 10, 14

cherry 21	icing 22	none 23	icing, cherry, sprinkles 24	none 25	icing 26	cherry 27	icing, sprinkles 28	none 29	icing, cherry 30
none 31	icing, sprinkles 32	cherry 33	icing 34	none 35	icing, cherry, sprinkles 36	none 37	icing 38	cherry 39	icing, sprinkles 40
none 41	icing, cherry 42	none 43	icing, sprinkles 44	cherry 45	icing 46	none 47	icing, cherry, sprinkles 48	none 49	icing 50

Pages 52–53 Pizza pie

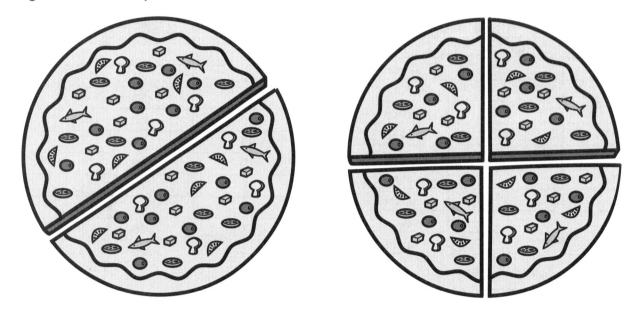

Pages 54–55 Making squares

Page 56 Moving the square

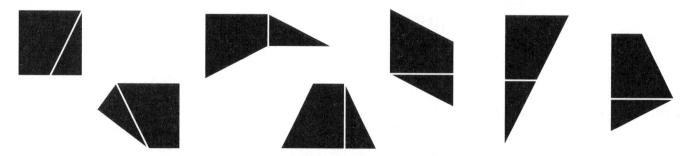